COPYRIGHT © 2019

All rights reserved.
No part of this publication
may be reproduced,
distributed or transmitted
in any form or by any means
including photocopying,
recording or other
electronic or mechanical
methods, without
the prior written
permission of the publisher,
except in the case
of brief quotations
embodied in critical reviews
and certain other
non commercial uses permitted
by copyright law.

Easter Coloring Book for Adults

THIS BOOK BELONGS TO:

_____

_____

_____

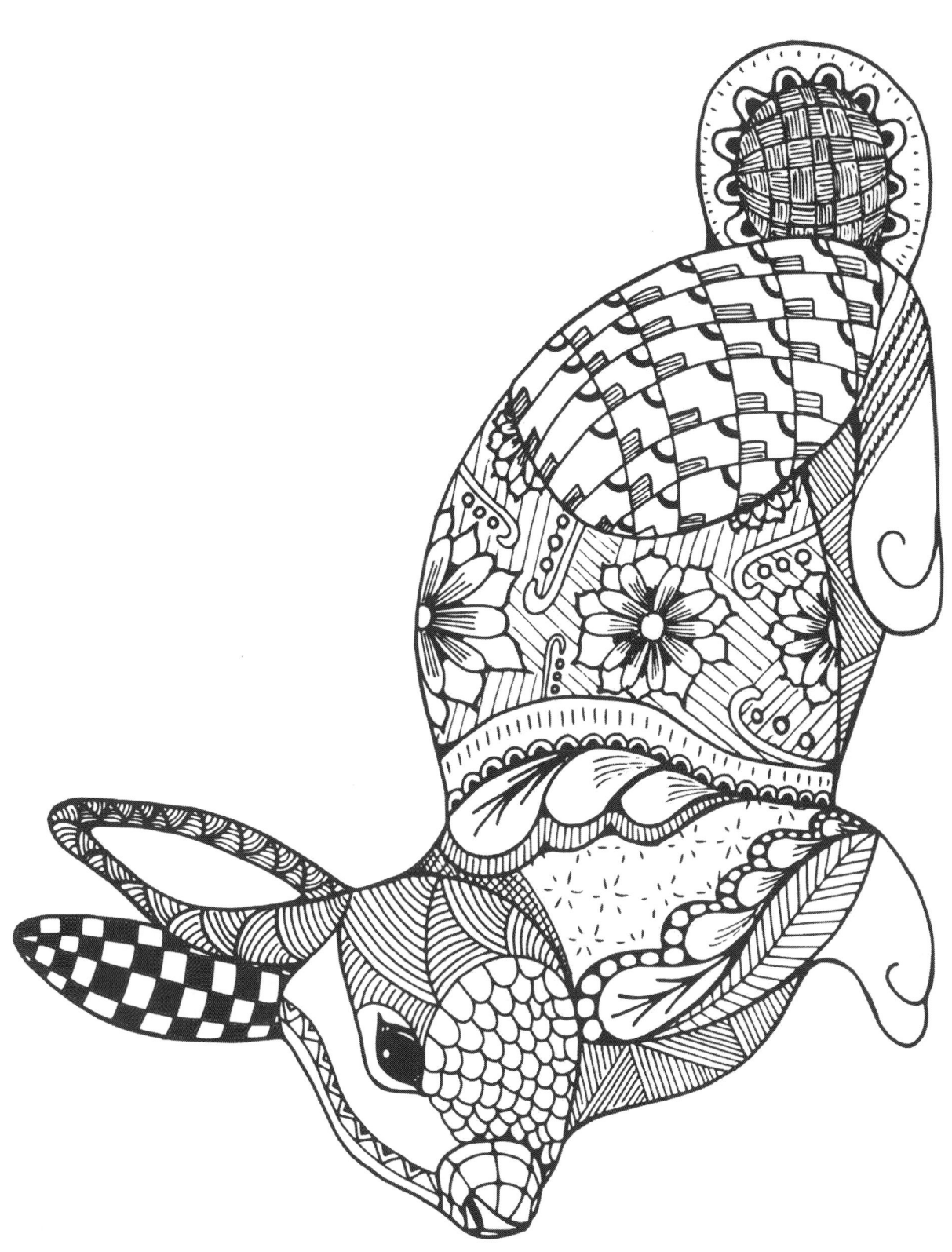

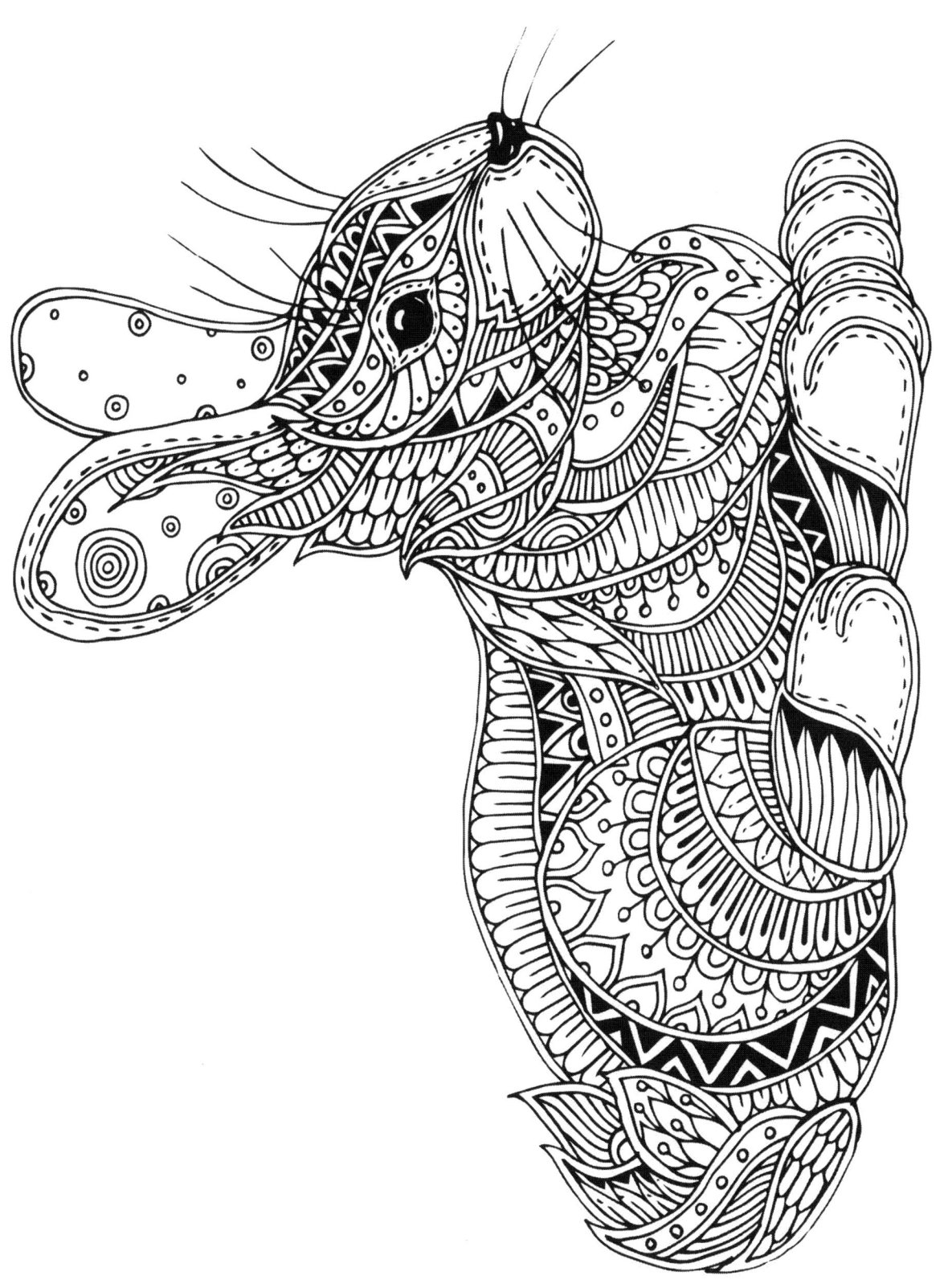

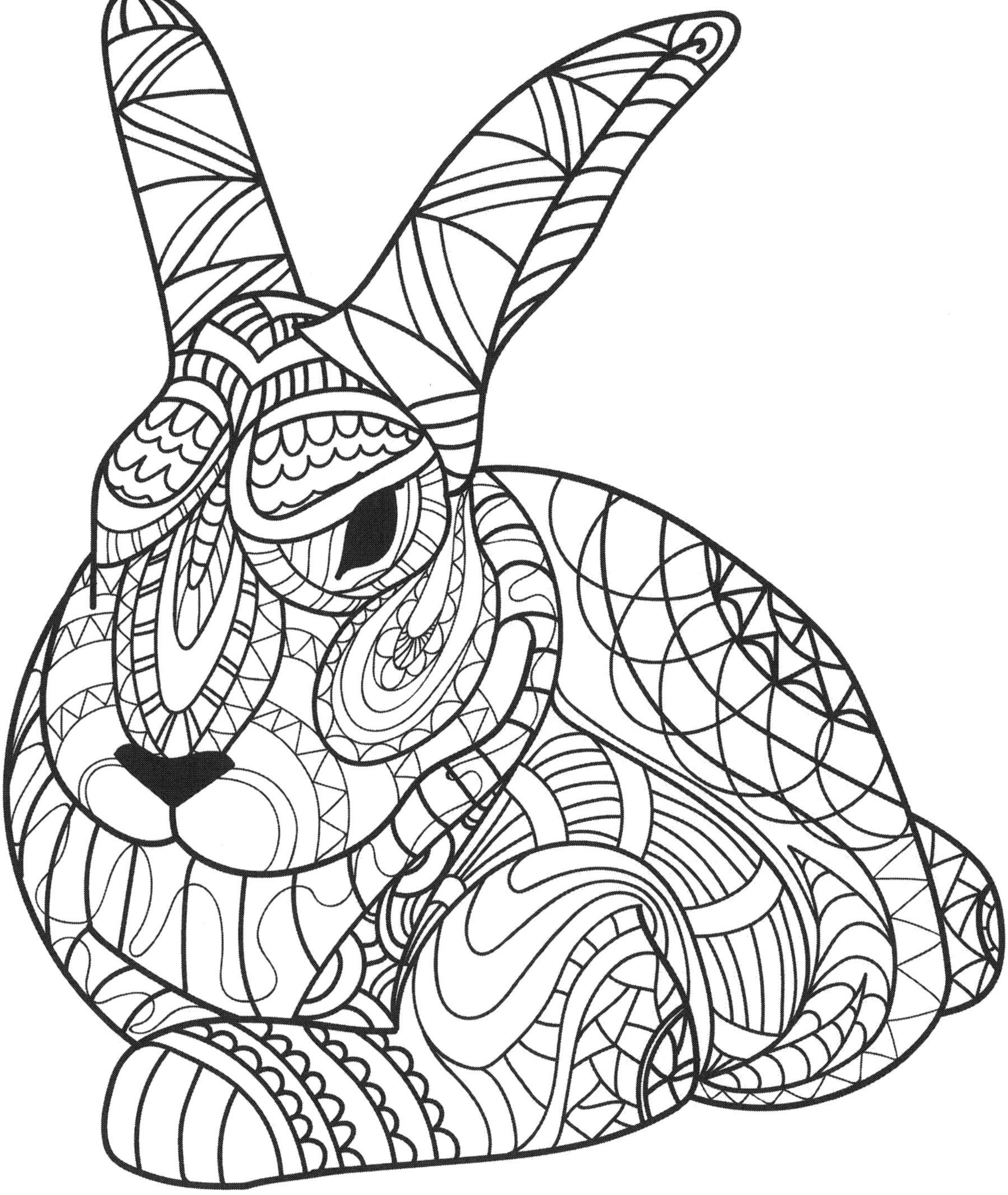

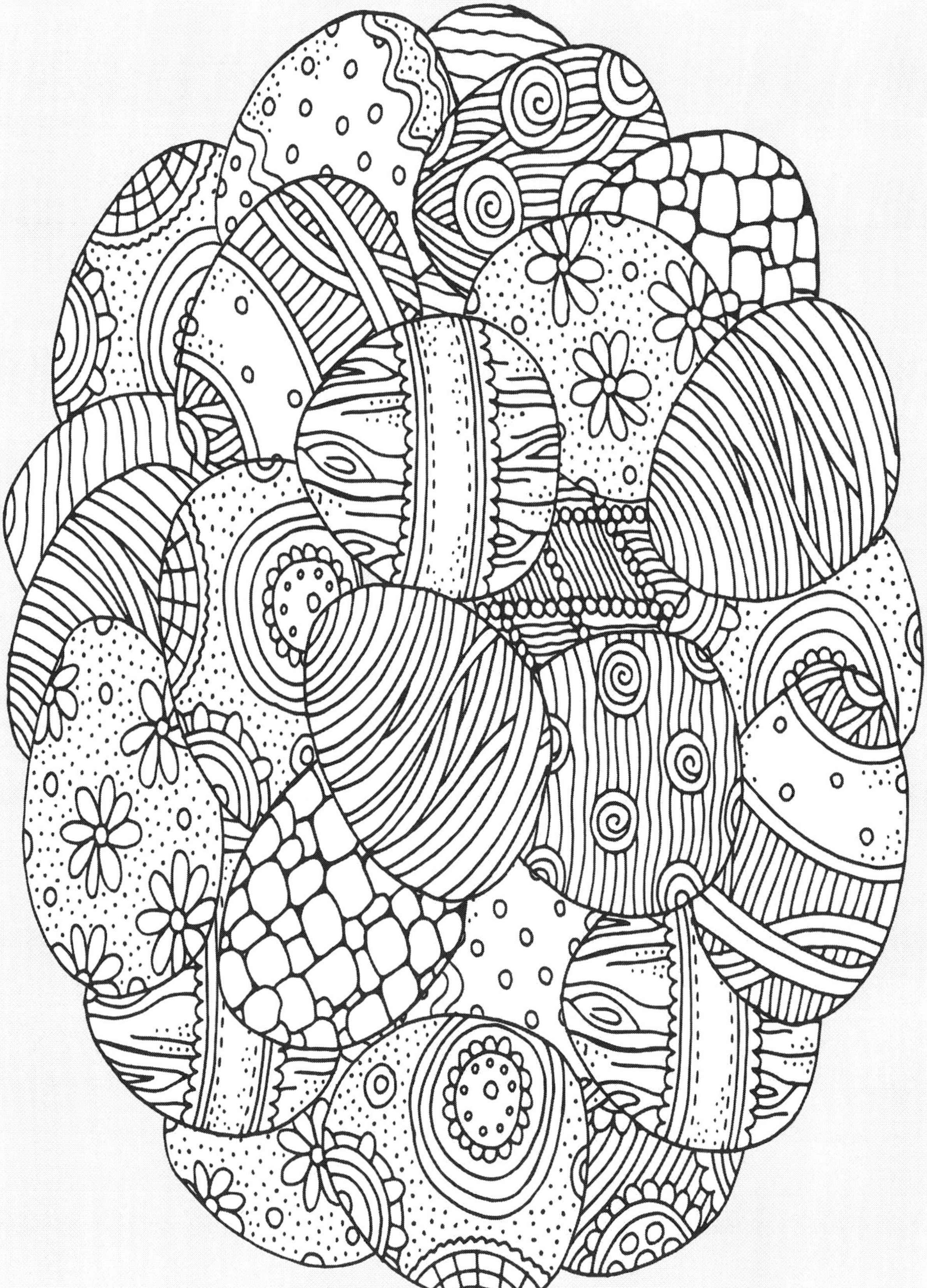

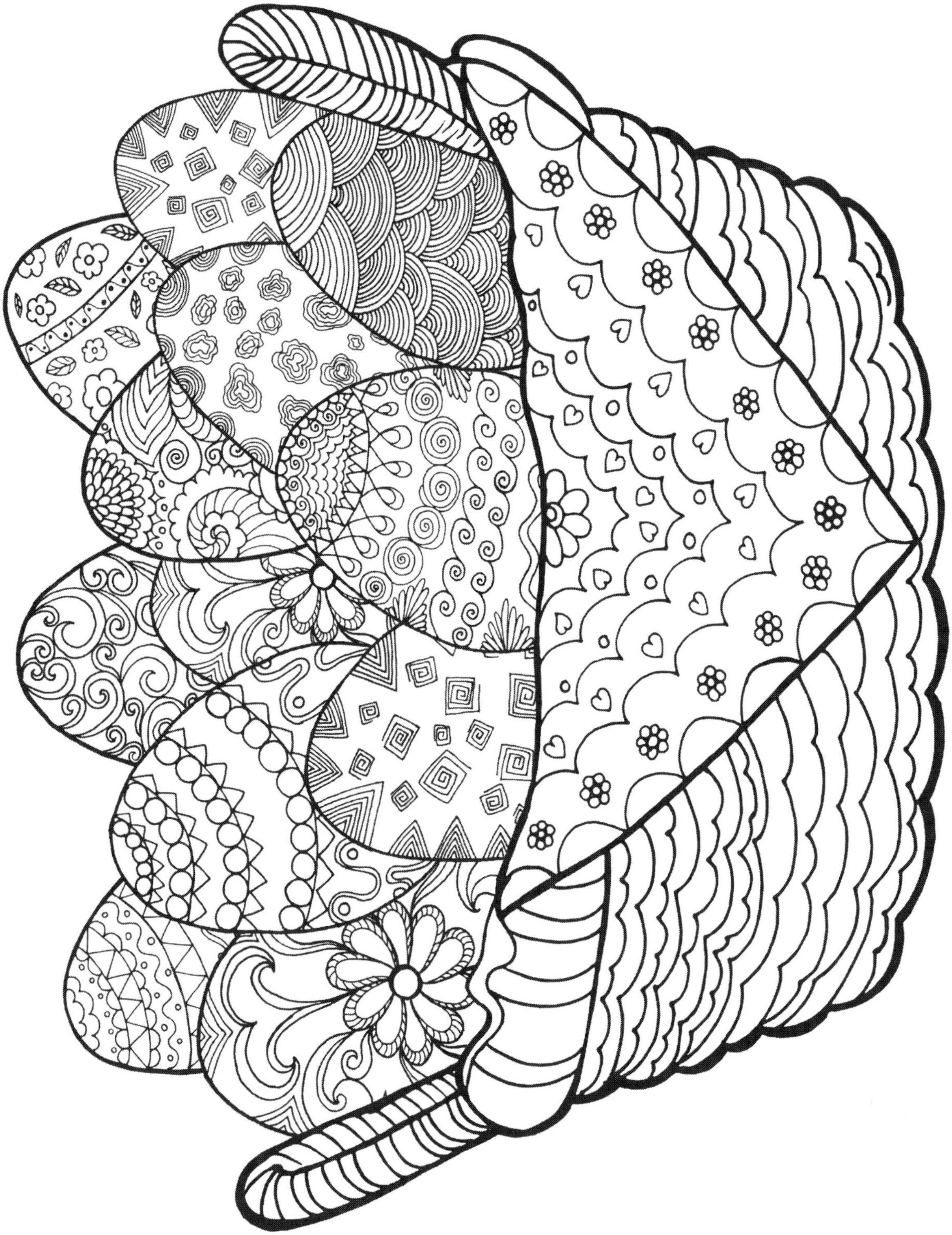

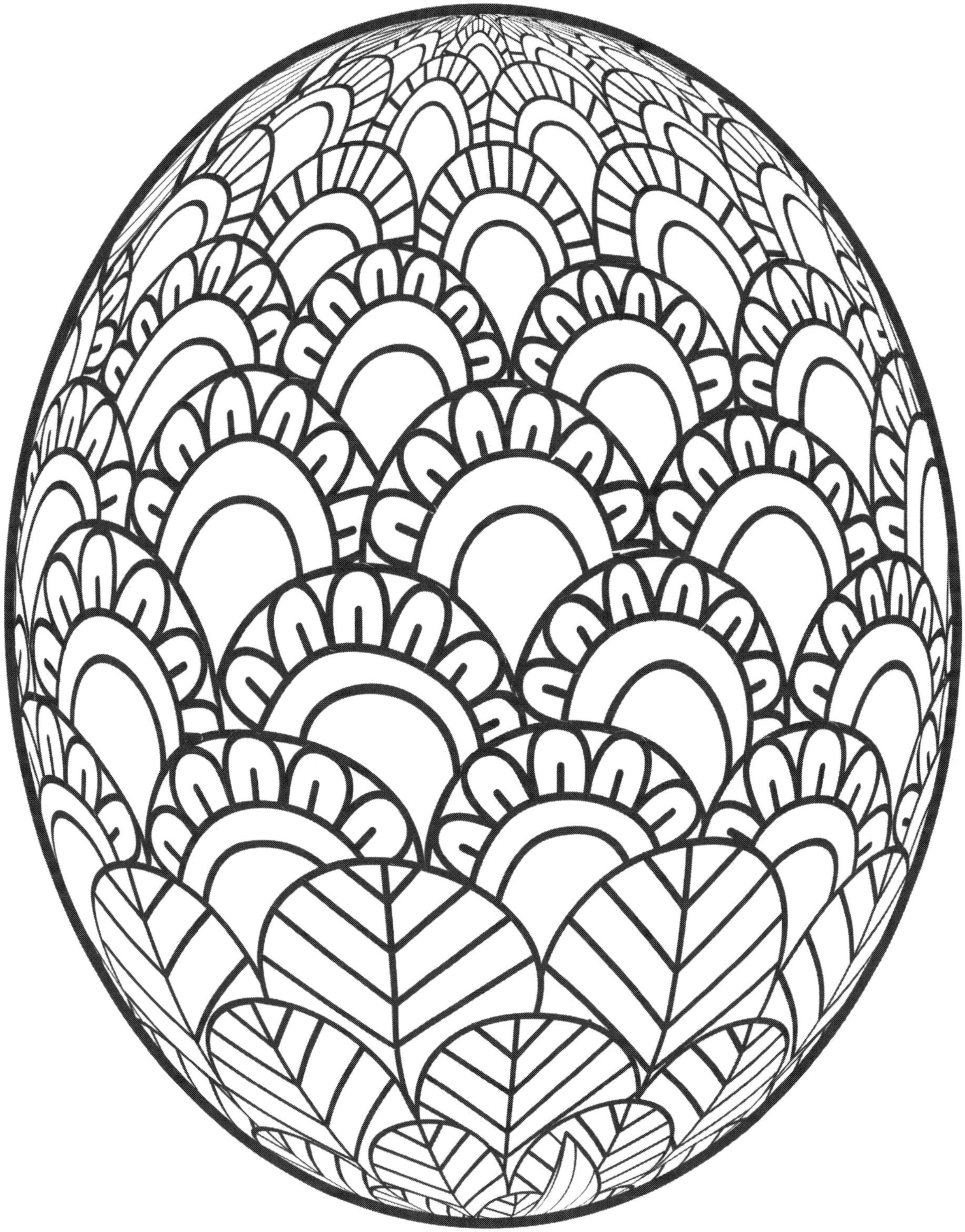

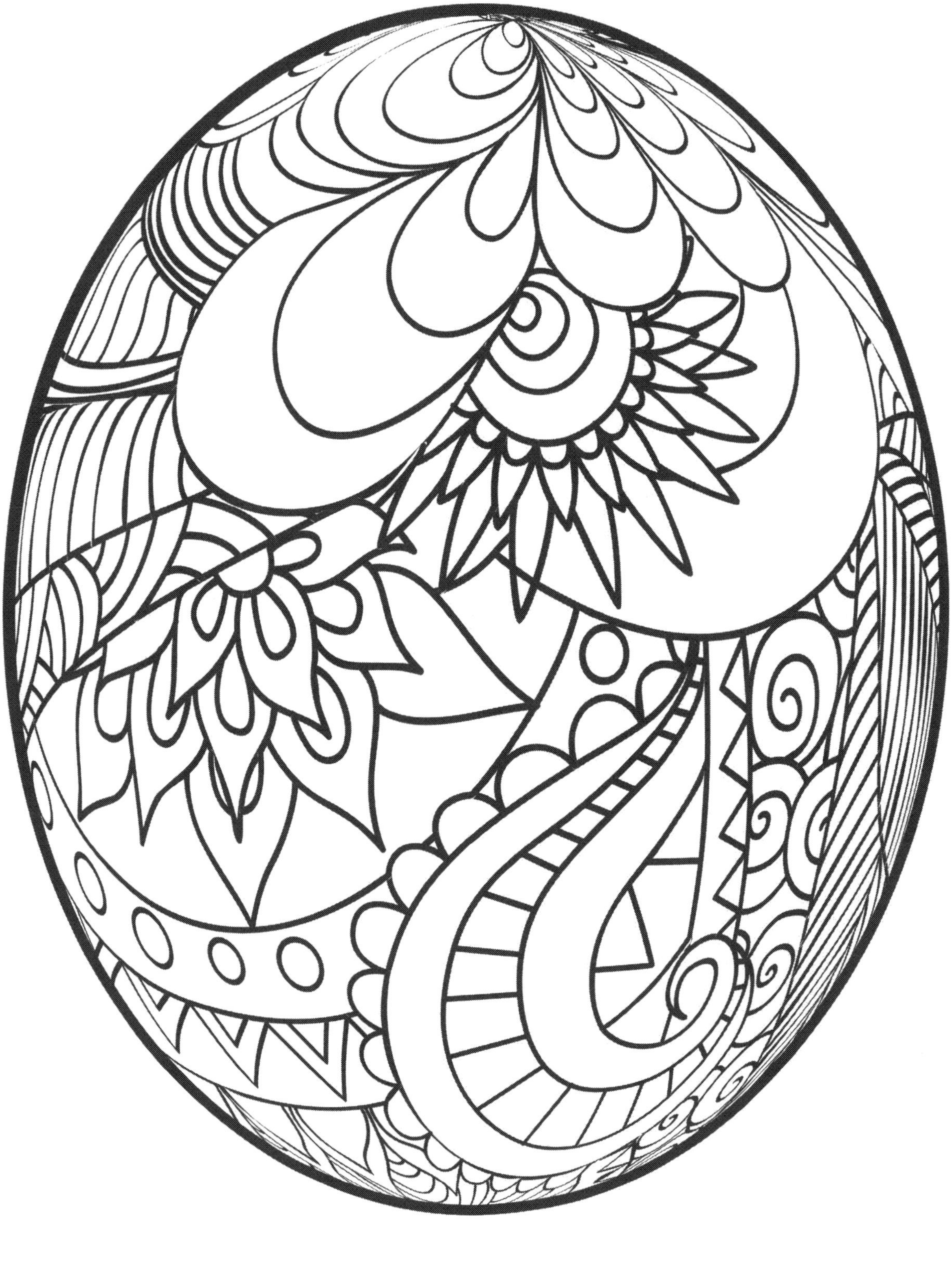

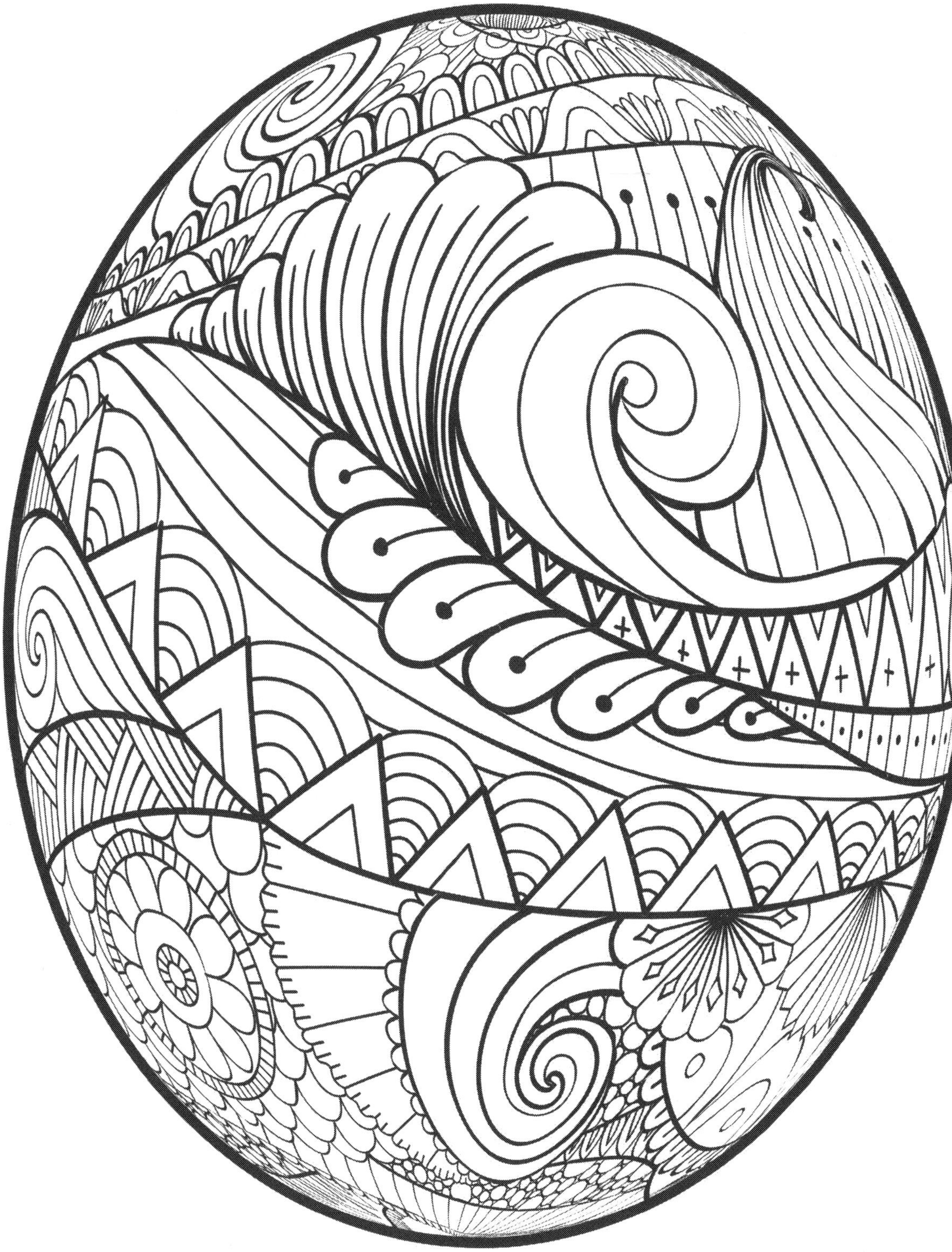

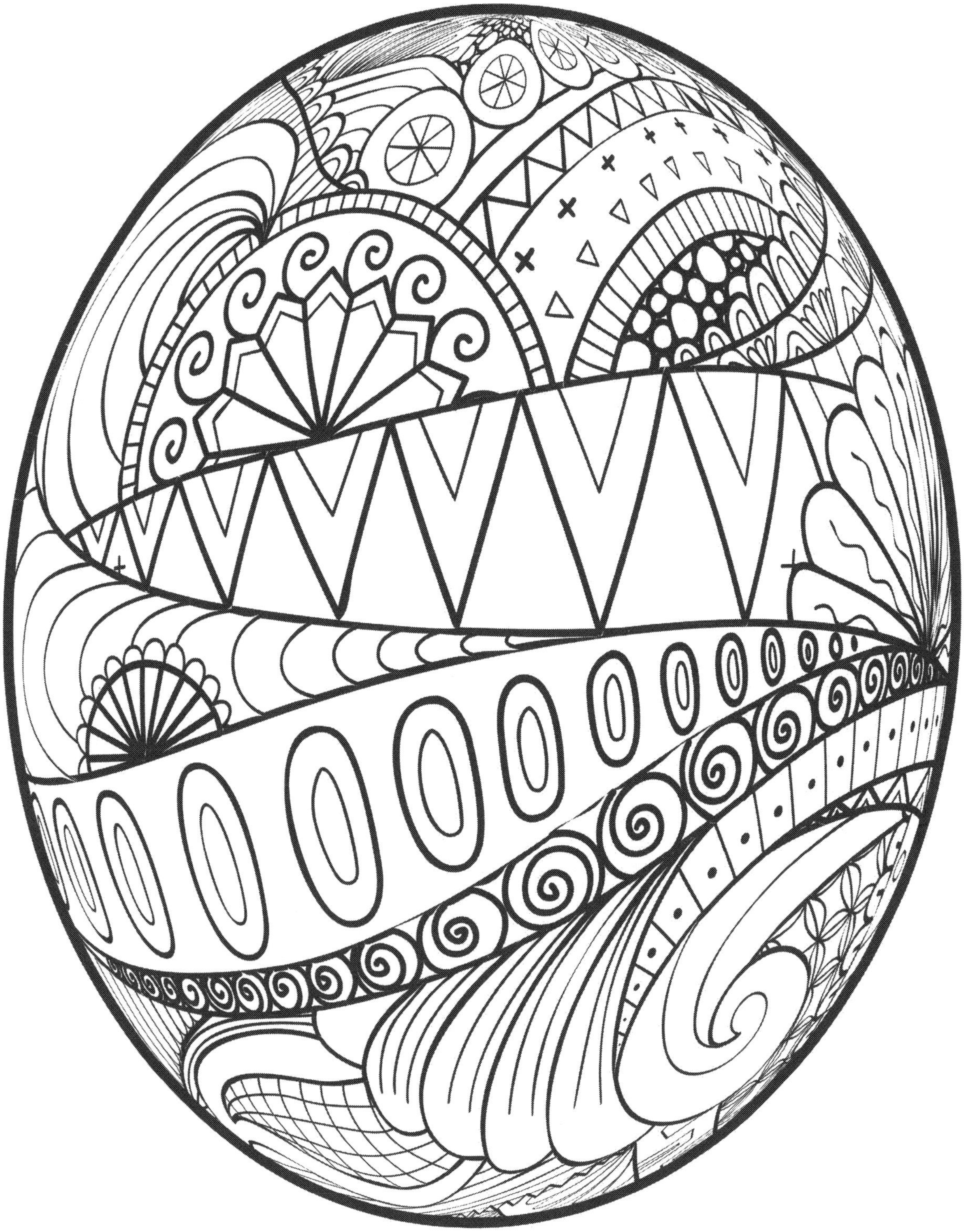

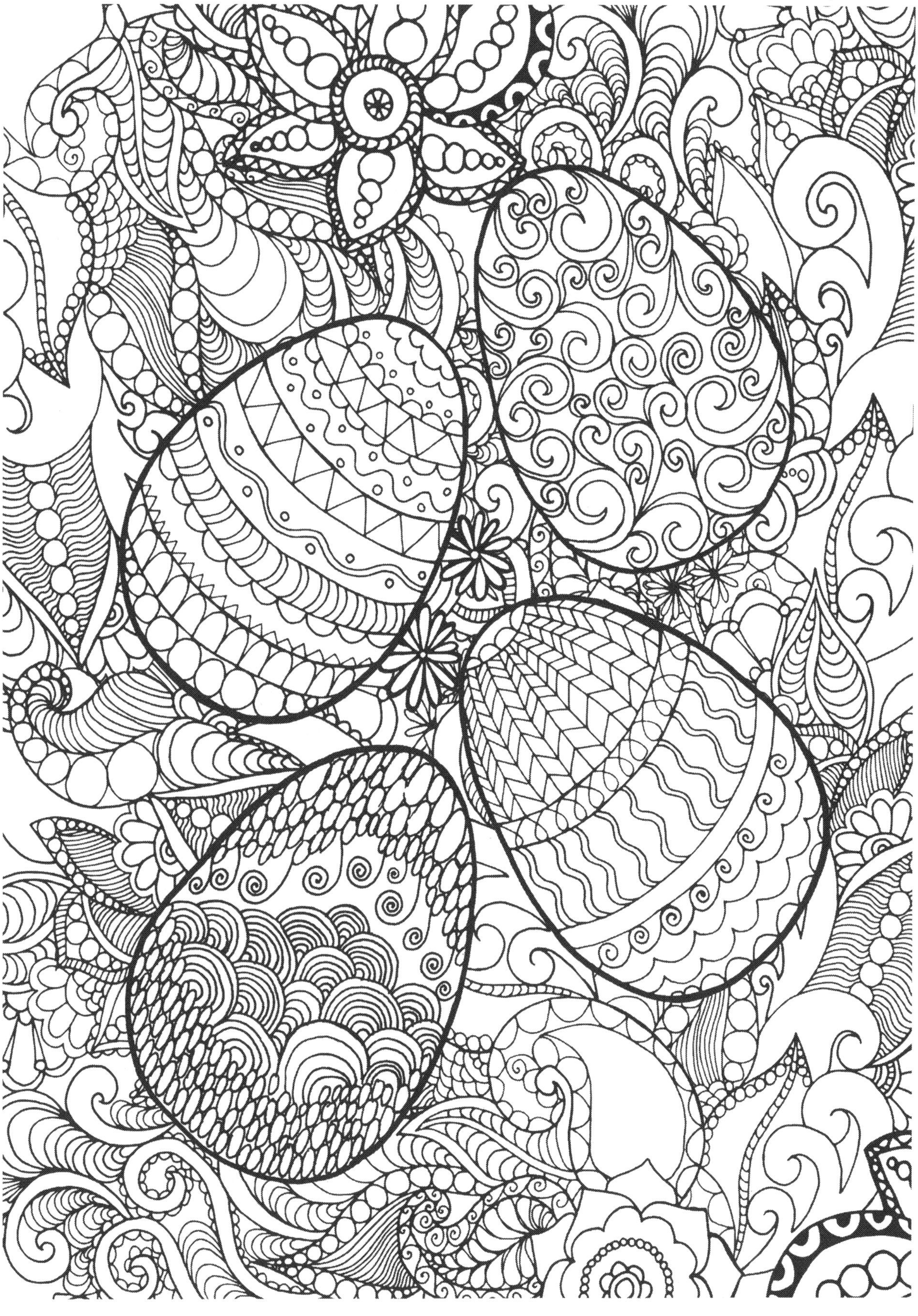

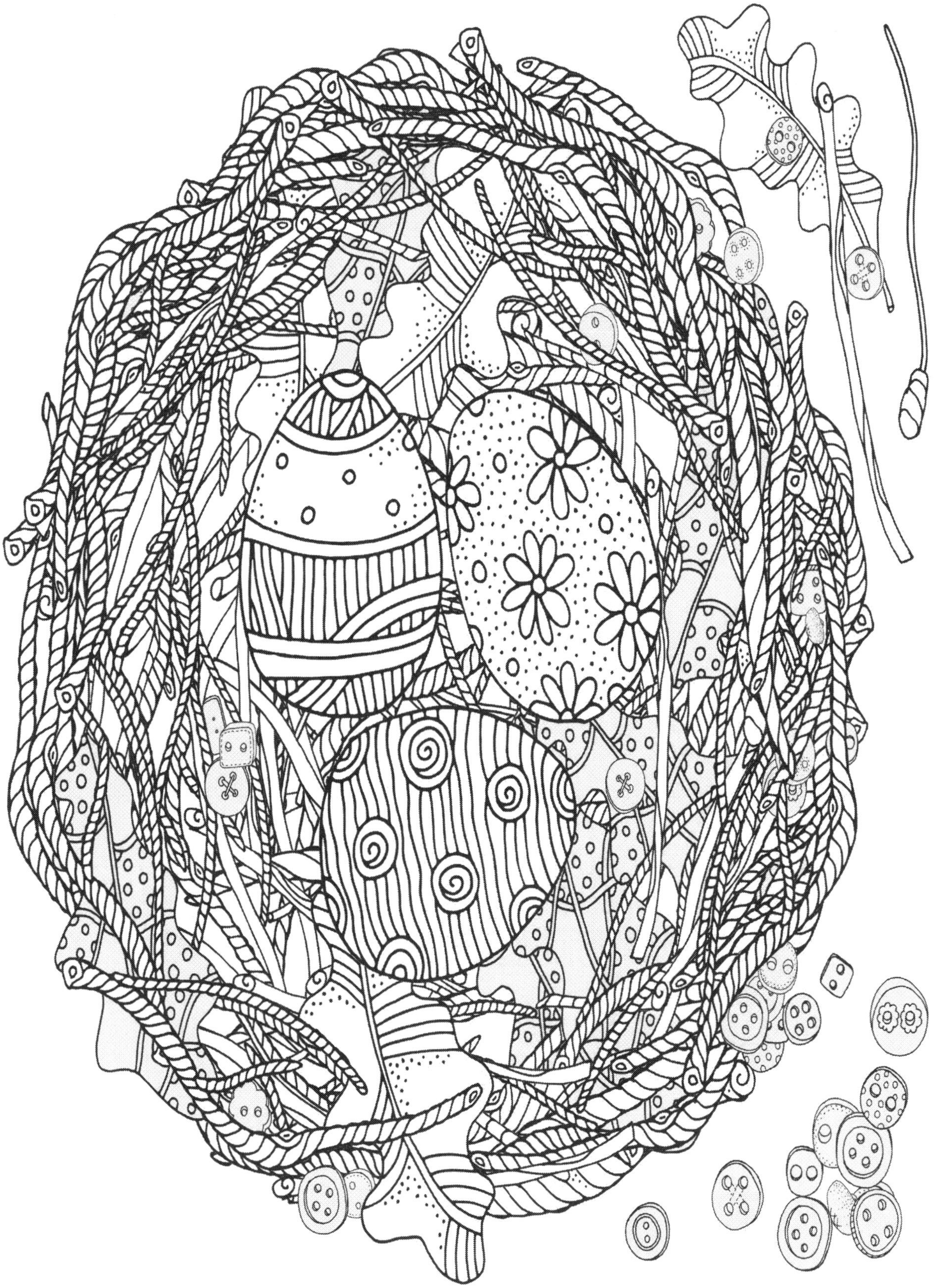

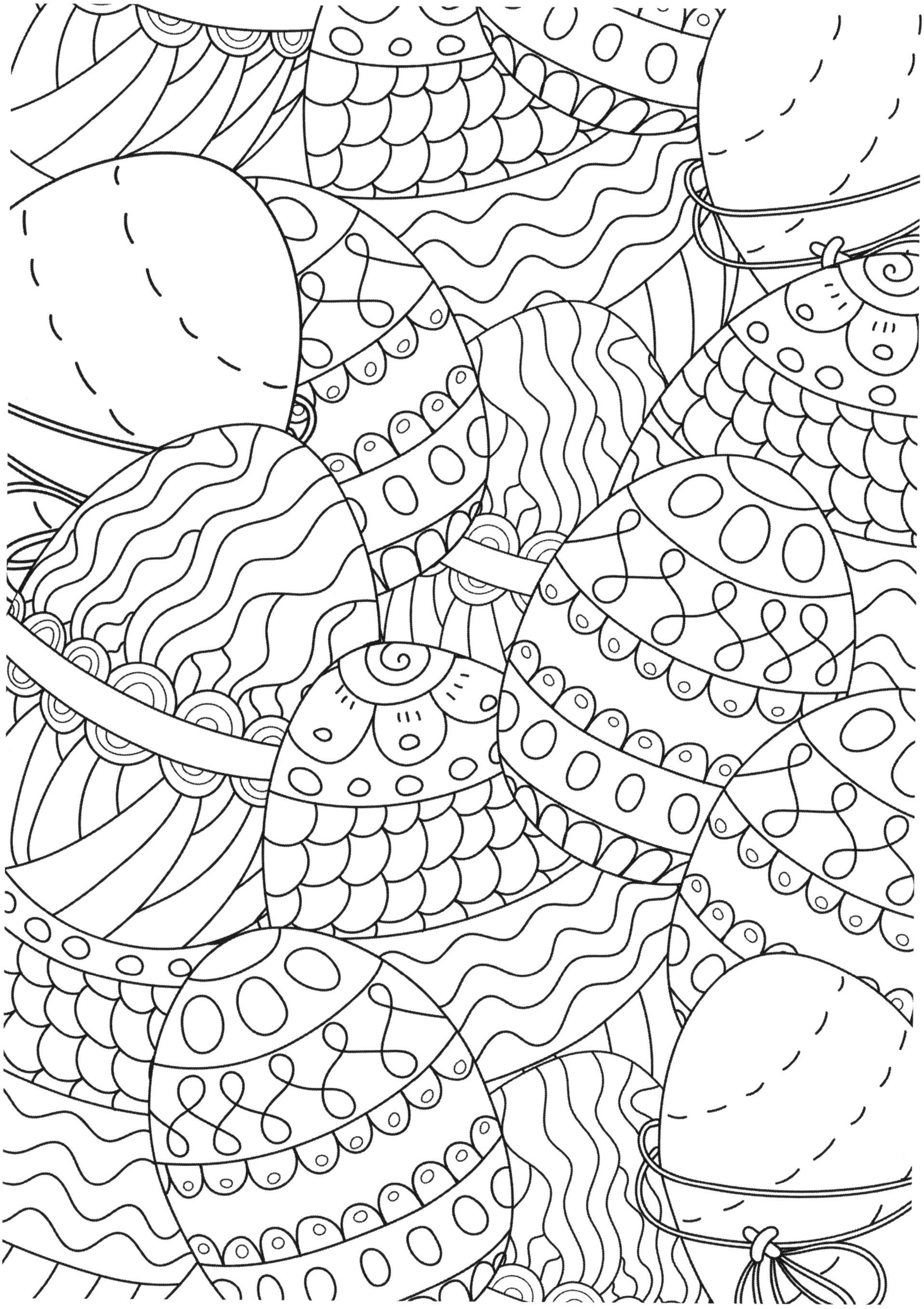

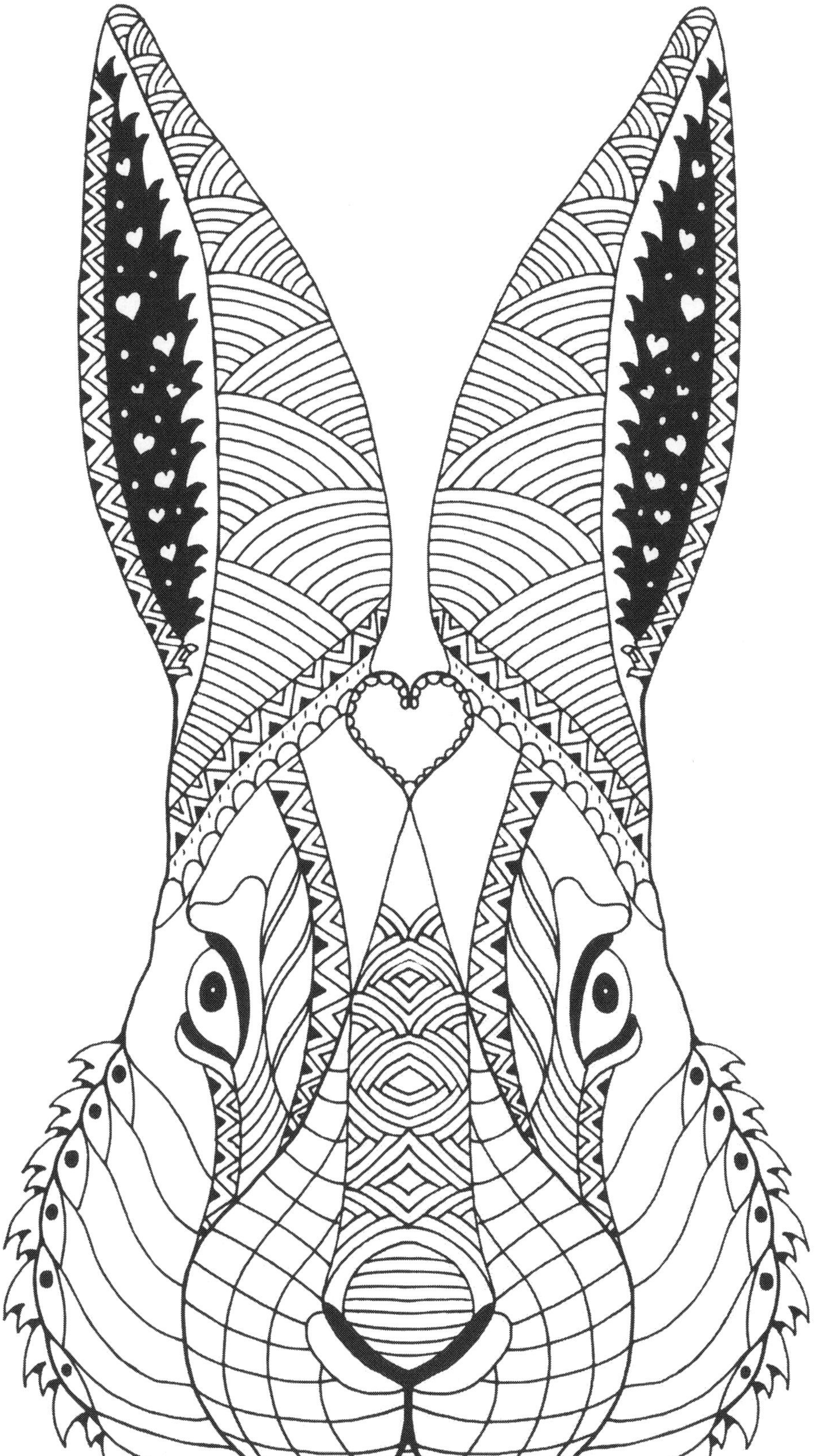

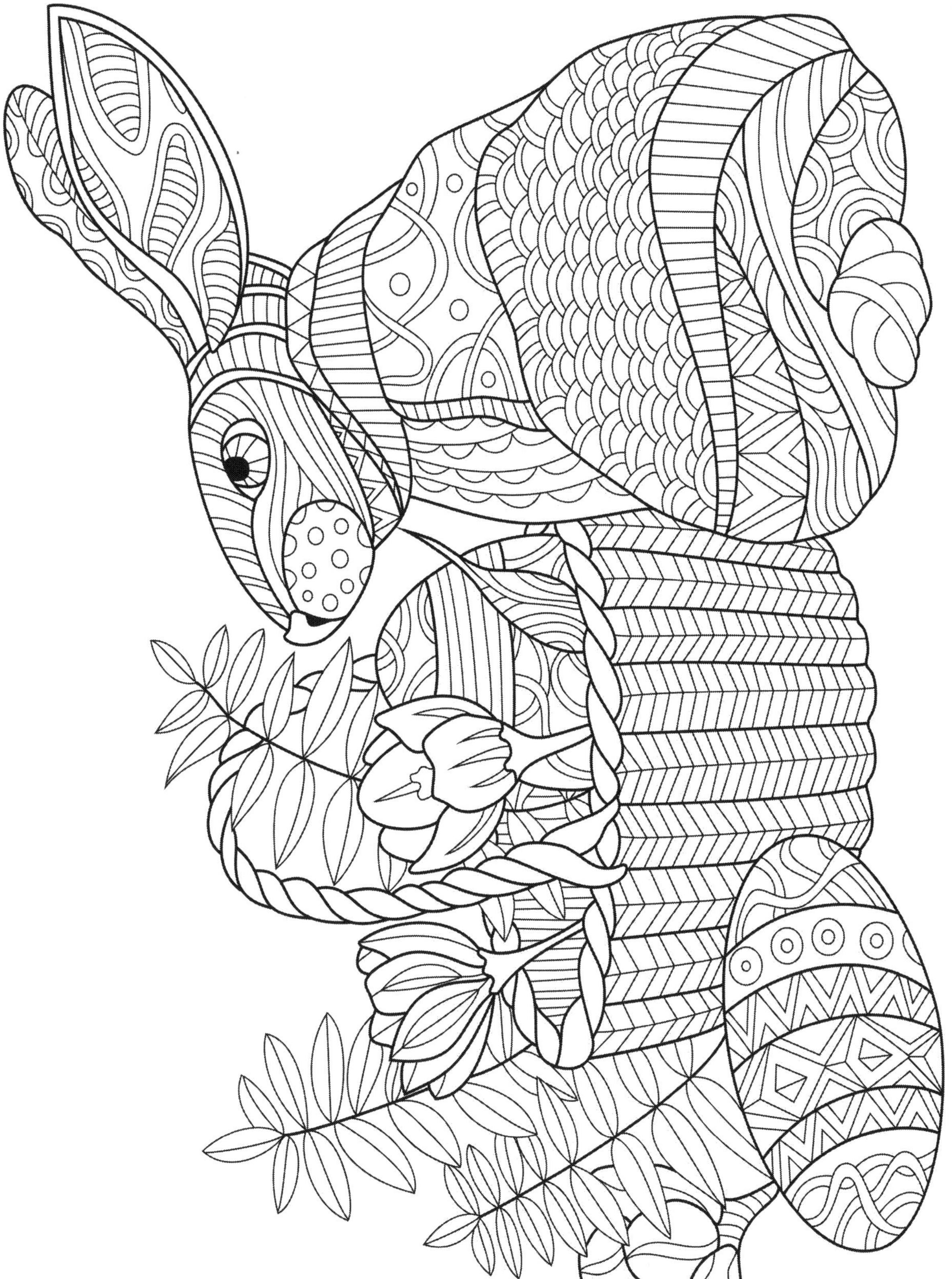

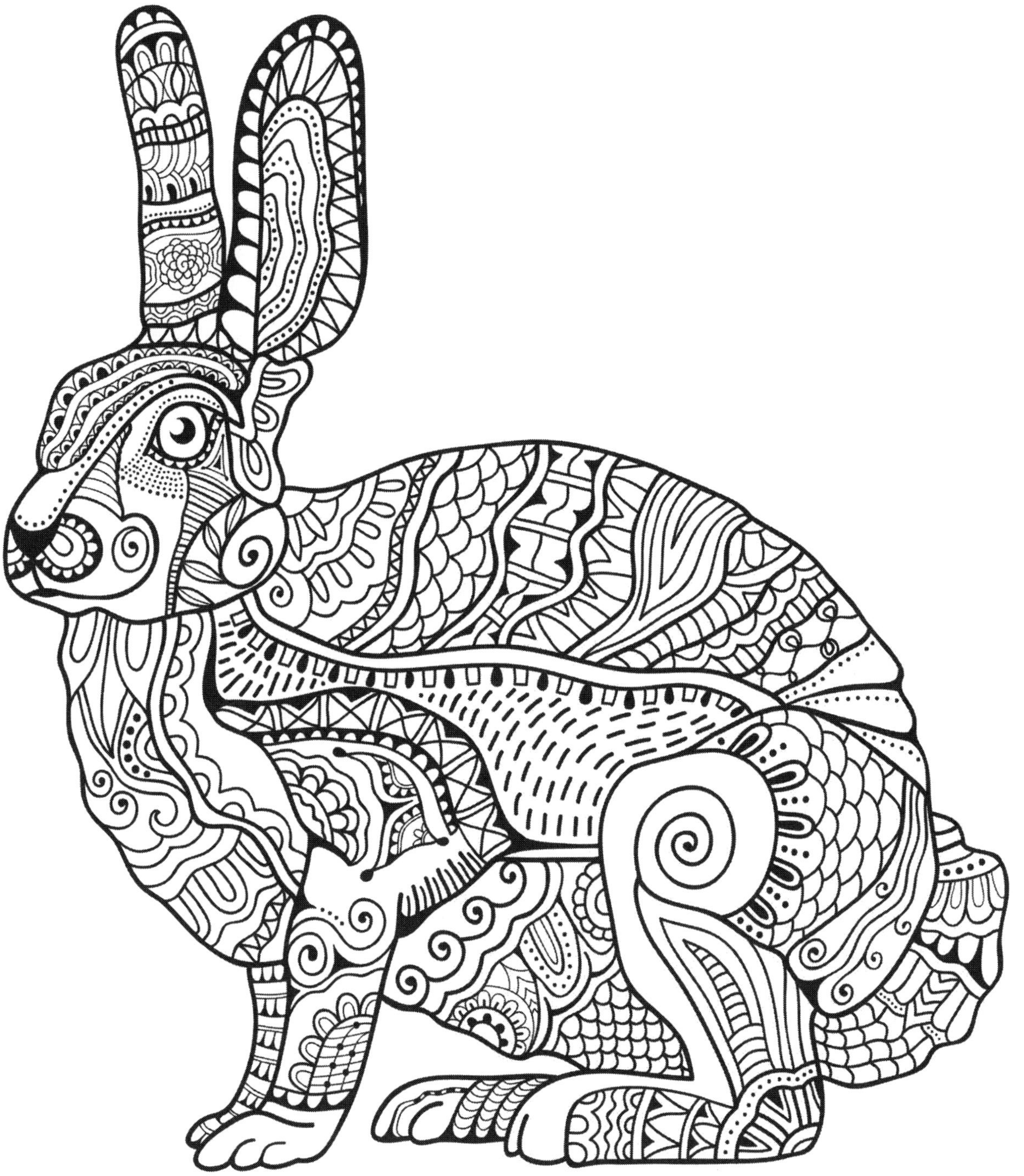

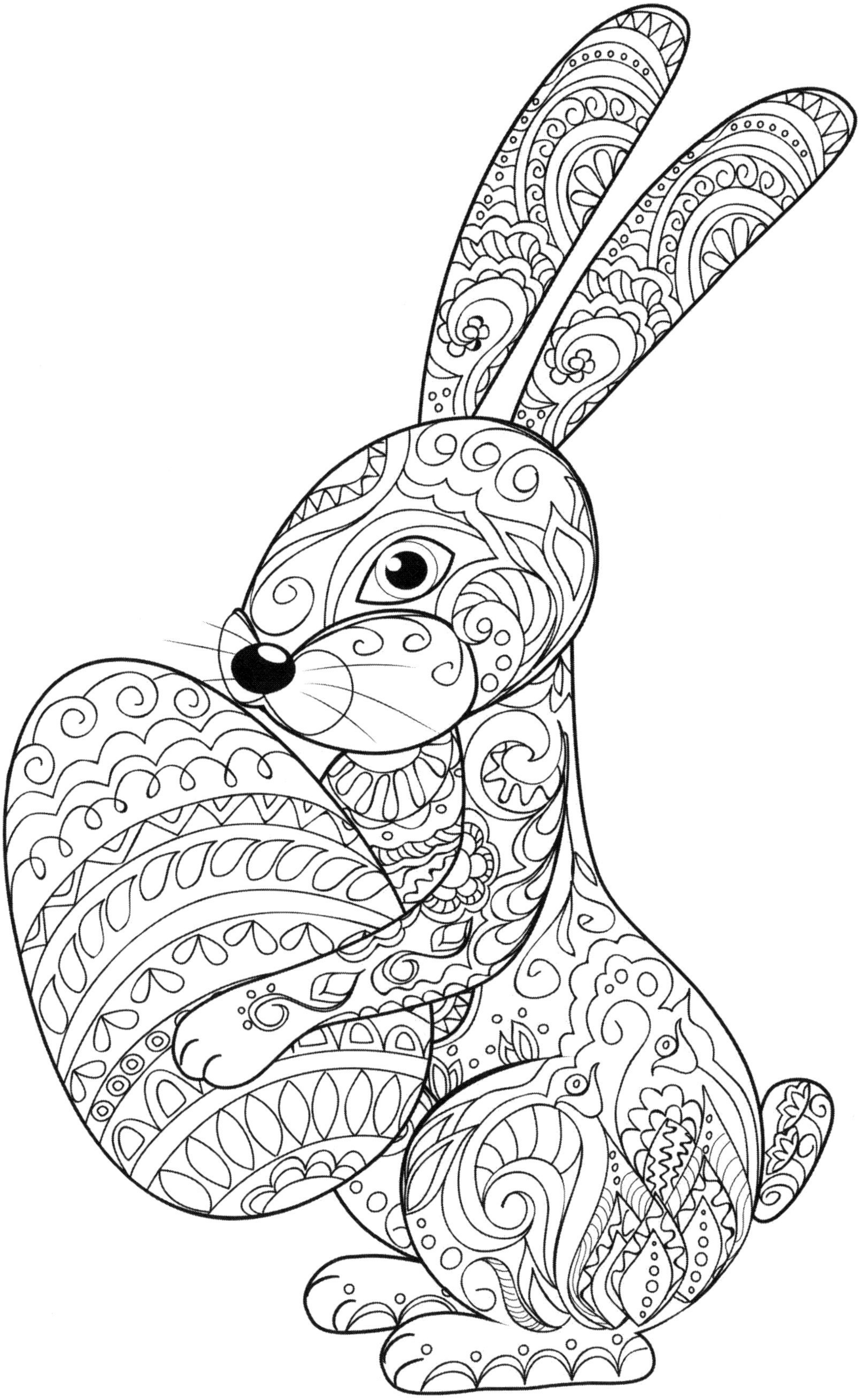

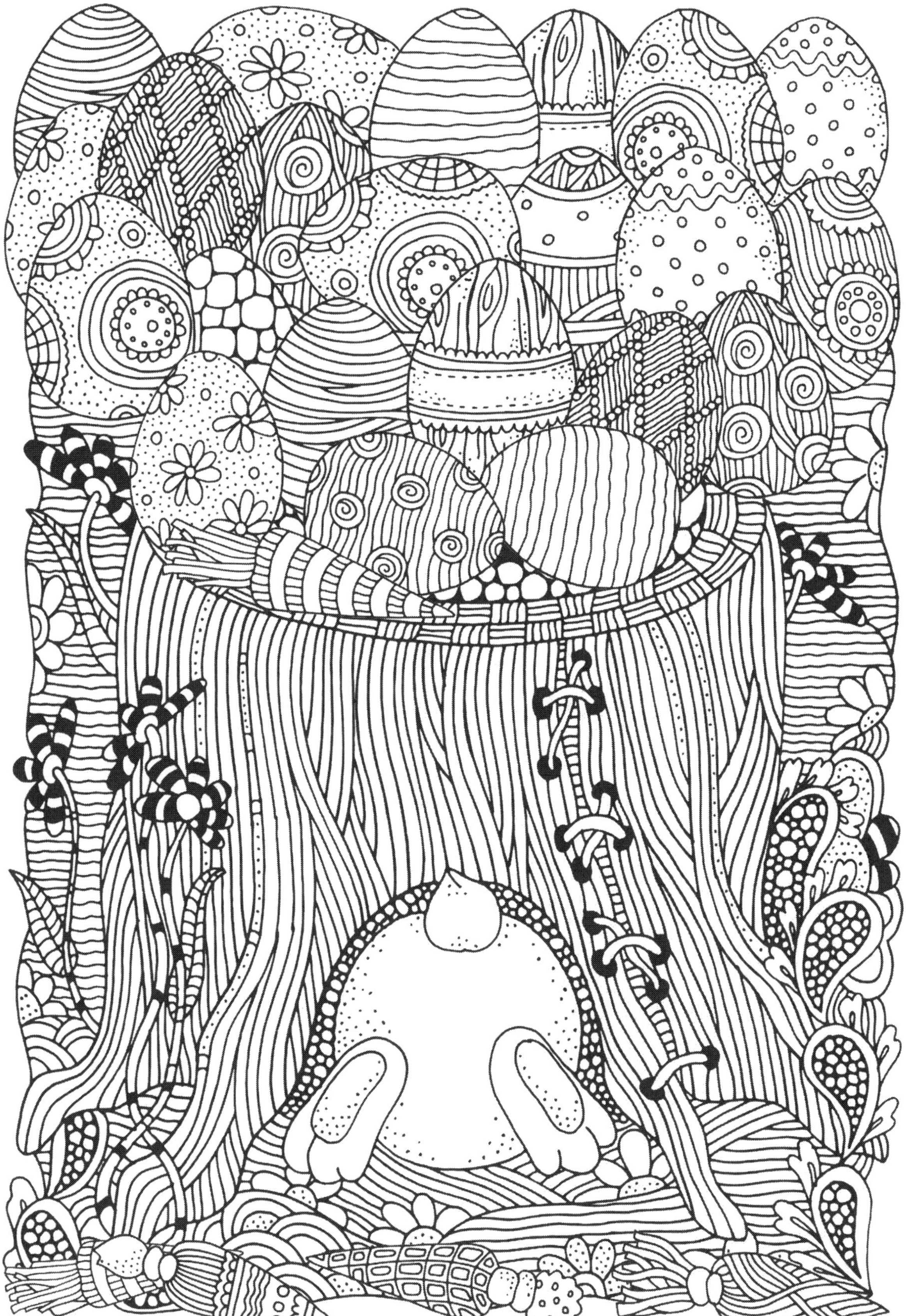

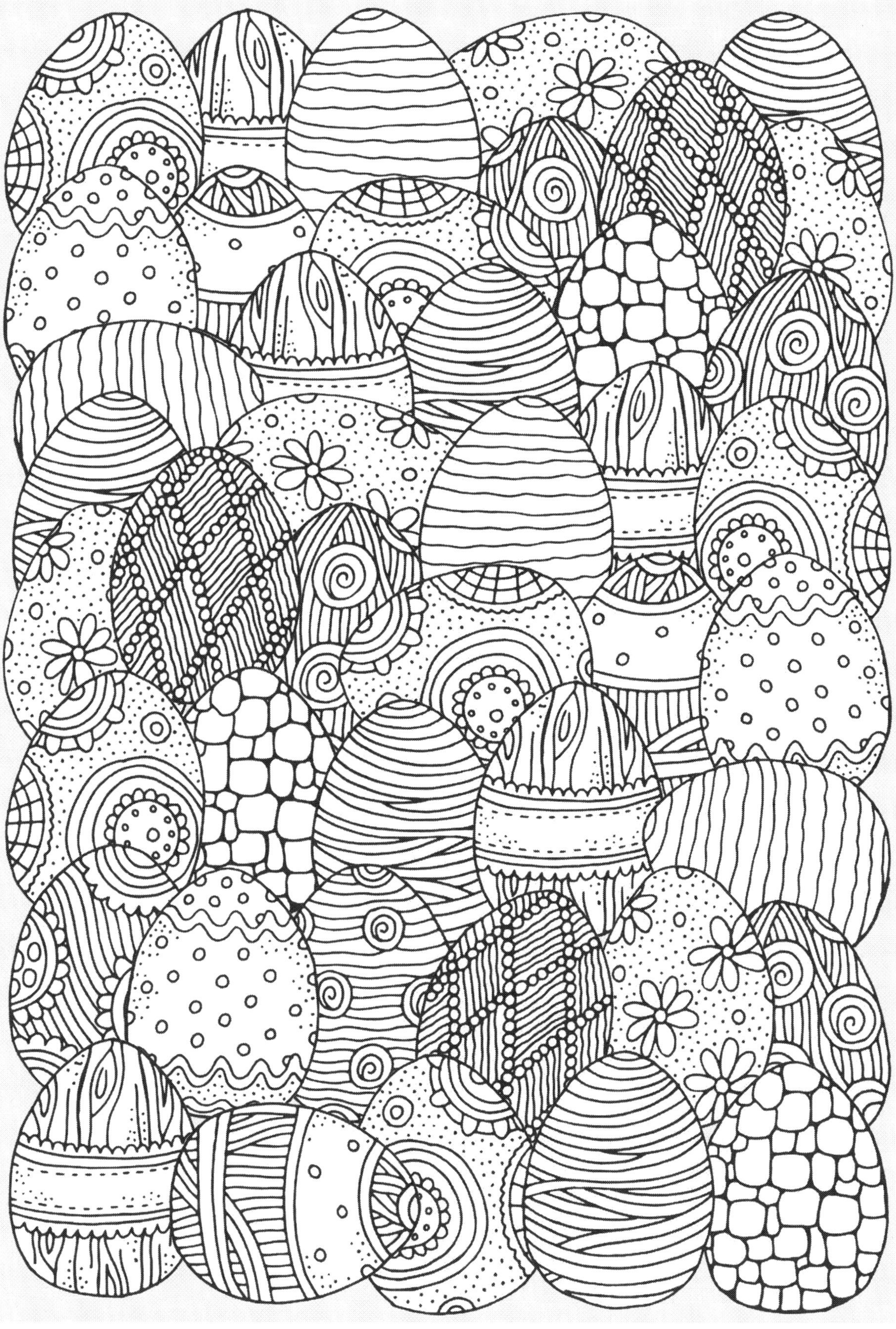

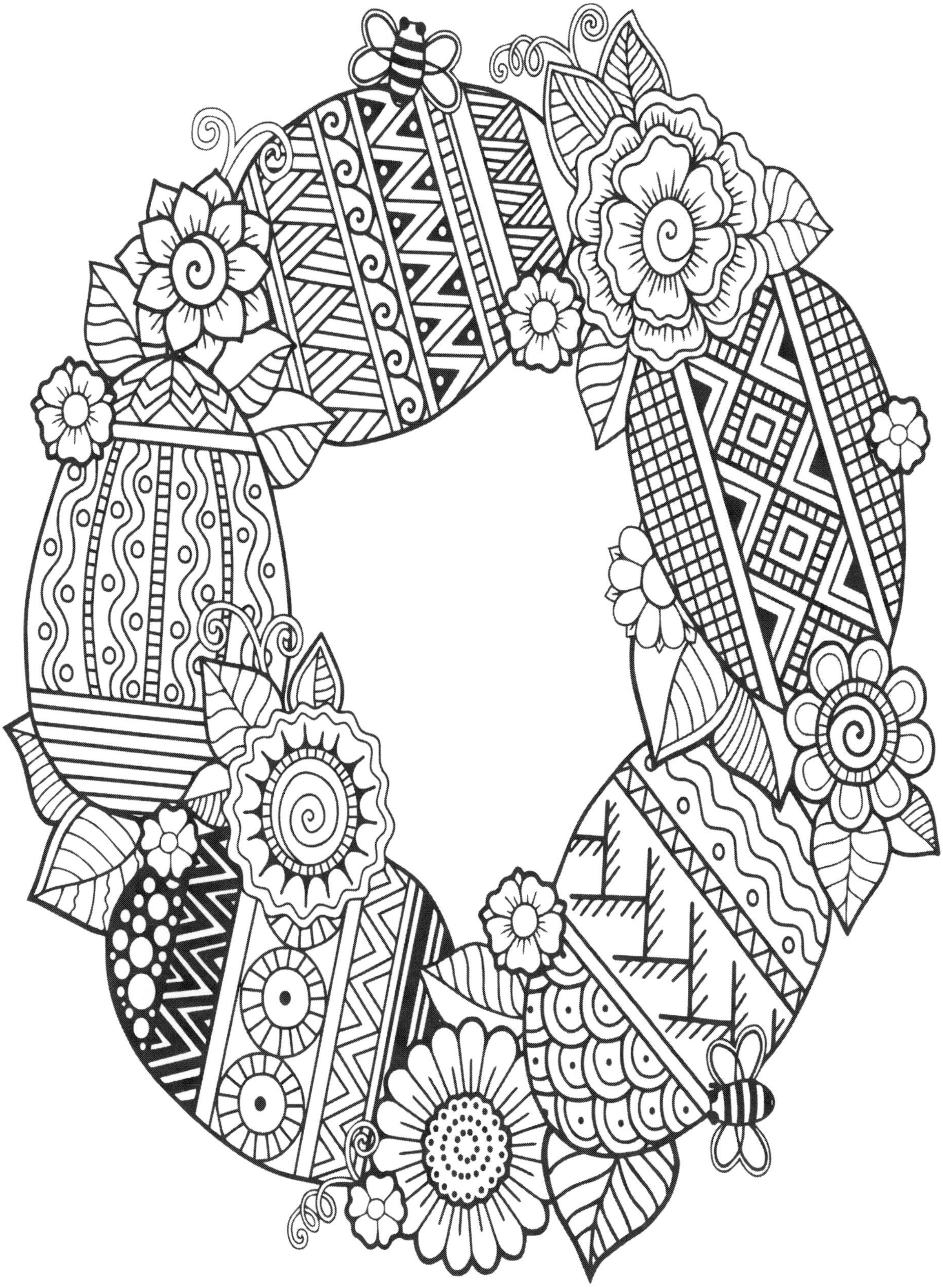

Made in the USA
Middletown, DE
16 March 2020